GEORGE
WASHINGTON

Military Heroes

GEORGE WASHINGTON
REVOLUTIONARY LEADER & FOUNDING FATHER

by Sari K. Earl

Content Consultant:
Brett Barker, Assistant Professor of History
University of Wisconsin–Marathon County

ABDO
Publishing Company

CREDITS

Published by ABDO Publishing Company, 8000 West 78th Street, Edina, Minnesota 55439. Copyright © 2010 by Abdo Consulting Group, Inc. International copyrights reserved in all countries. No part of this book may be reproduced in any form without written permission from the publisher. The Essential Library™ is a trademark and logo of ABDO Publishing Company.

Printed in the United States of America,
North Mankato, Minnesota
102009
012010

 PRINTED ON RECYCLED PAPER

Editor: Melissa Johnson
Copy Editor: Paula Lewis
Interior Design and Production: Kazuko Collins
Cover Design: Kazuko Collins

Library of Congress Cataloging-in-Publication Data
Earl, Sari.
  George Washington : revolutionary leader & founding father / Sari Earl.
     p. cm. — (Military heroes)
  Includes bibliographical references and index.
  ISBN 978-1-60453-967-7
  1. Washington, George, 1732-1799—Juvenile literature. 2. Generals—United States—Biography—Juvenile literature. 3. United States. Continental Army—Biography—Juvenile literature. 4. Presidents—United States—Biography—Juvenile literature. I. Title.

  E312.66.E25 2010
  973.4'1092--dc22
  [B]
                          2009032372

TABLE OF CONTENTS

*George Washington led the Continental army
during the American Revolution.*

"His Excellency"

On the night of October 5, 1781, the sky
was thick with rain clouds. They covered
the moon and filled the air with a cool mist. But
the heavy work of digging trenches kept the men
warm. The soldiers and workers of the bedraggled

Continental army dug relentlessly, trying to bring the trench line closer to the enemy. The Continental army was enmeshed in a war for the independence of the 13 American colonies from Great Britain. Often, it had seemed impossible that the Continental army could win the war. Now, however, they had the British forces trapped. The war for independence had reached Yorktown, in Virginia. General Charles Cornwallis and his British troops were quartered near the Continental army, and the leader of the Continental army, General George Washington, intended victory at last. With his forces impeding Cornwallis's escape by land and the French fleet blocking a retreat by water, Cornwallis was trapped. The siege at Yorktown had begun. The trenches would allow the Continental army to get close enough to fire artillery at the British army.

The Famous Face

Appearing today on the one-dollar bill, George Washington's face is well recognized around the world. Washington was tall, particularly for his time, when people tended to be shorter than they are today. From his portraits, many people think that Washington wore a wig. In fact, he wore his hair tied back and powdered, which was the style during his time.

Many people believe that Washington's teeth were made out of wood. Washington did suffer from dental disease and probably owned more than one set of false teeth. However, instead of wood, they were likely crafted from hippopotamus ivory, animal teeth, metal, and springs. They were probably uncomfortable and may have even distorted his mouth, causing the grimace seen in many of his portraits.

As Washington's men dug, they tried not to think about the British sentries close by. They all knew that if the enemy discovered them, they likely would be killed.

His Excellency

Washington watched the work. At more than six feet (1.8 m) tall, he stood well above most of the men. He was broad shouldered, with a striking military bearing. His hair was pulled back from his face, exposing wide eyes and a mouth that always seemed tense. He had an air of authority, and the other officers treated him with exceptional deference. He was the only man referred to as "His Excellency" in the Continental army.

A Farmer and a Slave Owner

When people think of George Washington, they think of him as a general, a commander, and the first president of the United States. Some are surprised to learn that he took great pleasure in being a farmer. Many of his surviving letters deal with crops and farming issues. Washington owned a plantation in Virginia.

At that time, plantations typically were worked by slaves. Washington inherited and owned slaves, as did many other early presidents from the South. He made a provision in his will for some slaves to be freed after his and his wife's deaths. Washington did not speak much publicly or write at length about slavery. However, other men in Washington's social position took quicker steps to free their slaves during this time, when they realized slavery conflicted with the ideals of the American Revolution.

These men in the Continental army were farmers and woodsmen and clerks, not professional soldiers. They wore homemade uniforms, and many left the service as soon as their commitments were completed, leaving Washington with an ever-changing army. Washington's untrained army faced the most feared fighting force in the world. Nevertheless, he led with energy and purpose. For six hard years, he had fought for their freedom. Now, with Cornwallis trapped, Washington was ready to do whatever was necessary for victory.

The Cherry Tree

In one famous story, George Washington used a hatchet to chop down a cherry tree when he was a small boy. When his father asked George what had happened to the tree, George supposedly confessed, saying that he could not tell a lie. Little information is known about George's early childhood or his relationship with his father. In fact, this story was made up by Parson Mason Weems, who wrote one of the first biographies of the great leader. The tale was used to show that, from a very young age, Washington was honest, no matter the consequences.

ENDING THE WAR

In the ditch, the general was vulnerable to British attack. If he were caught, it could mean the end of the war for independence. Indeed, Washington often had been in the heart of danger without suffering even a scratch. Enemy soldiers had fired muskets at him at close range. He had led charges into battle and seen men fall all around him.

Washington watched the men the night of October 5 and returned again October 6 with a pickaxe. Washington's presence in the trenches was partly symbolic. The Patriots sensed that the war was coming to a close, so Washington took personal control of some of the last military actions. With ceremony, he drove his pickaxe into the ground. Although the men had already started to dig, he wanted history to show that he had "with his own hands first broke ground at the siege of Yorktown."[1]

When the trench lines were finally close enough to the enemy on October 9, Washington fired the first cannon at the British camp. Legend tells that his cannonball bounced right through a group of British officers eating dinner. From that point, the cannon shots did not cease until the British surrendered on October 17, 1781. Although General Cornwallis gave up his sword on October 19, Washington would not know for several months that the war was actually over. He still feared that the British would continue to send troops. He urged the Continental Congress to let him attack other cities held by British forces. When the British king learned of Cornwallis's defeat, however, he decided to stop fighting. "It is all over," the king told his advisors.[2]

Washington helped build the trenches at Yorktown, Virginia,
where the British were defeated.

George's mother did not want him to choose a military career.

A CHILD OF VIRGINIA

eorge Washington was born to Augustine and Mary Ball Washington on February 22, 1732. Mary was Augustine's second wife. The Washingtons had lived in Virginia for generations. Augustine fathered three children with his first wife, who had died three years earlier. George was born in Westmoreland County, Virginia. He soon had four younger siblings, too. In 1743, when George was 11, Augustine died, leaving Mary Ball with seven children, a large estate, and slaves.

Even as a boy, George was tall. He had grayish blue eyes and brown hair that he tied back. George's education began with a tutor. However, unlike his older half brothers and many other young men from wealthy families, George never attended a university or studied in Europe. He lost the opportunity because his father died and his mother did not want him to leave home. Later in life, George seemed to regret having missed out on a formal education.

George also spent a lot of time with Lawrence, his half brother. Lawrence was approximately 14 years older than George and lived nearby at an estate called Mount Vernon. George looked up to his half brother, who became almost a second father to him. Lawrence was a military officer in the Virginia military, which was under the command of the British army. When George was 14, Lawrence suggested that George join the British navy, but Mary Ball said no. George's military career would not begin for several more years.

SURVEYOR

When George was 15, he started spending more time at Mount Vernon with Lawrence and his wife, Ann Fairfax. Ann was from a well-regarded Virginian family who owned a lot of land. At 16, George began his first job. The Fairfax family hired him to assist a team that was surveying their land holdings. He had to find his way through forests and mountains, walking the boundaries of people's new properties and mapping the rivers and other features. George traveled west of the Blue Ridge Mountains into the Ohio Valley, where he saw American Indians and settlers. He gained experience traveling in rugged country and meeting with

Rules of Civility

Many historians have focused on a document that George copied during his childhood, *The Rules of Civility and Decent Behaviour in Company and Conversation*. The document might have been a list of rules that George copied to exercise his penmanship or perhaps a means of learning rules of etiquette. Scholars believe that George was about 16 at the time.

George was known for his good manners. Some historians believe that George used these rules as a guide in his public and private lives. An example of a rule about general behavior reads, "Every Action done in Company, ought to be with Some Sign of Respect, to those that are Present."[1] The 110 rules include: do not kill fleas or vermin in front of others; do not leave your room half-dressed; do not cross your feet when sitting; do not laugh too loudly; keep your teeth clean; do not speak with your mouth full of food; and associate with polite, good people because it is better to be alone than to be in bad company.

indigenous peoples. He kept a diary of the expedition. In his entry of March 15, 1748, George gave an indication of some of the hardships he faced. He wrote about the sleeping situations, describing the bed as:

> . . . nothing but a Little Straw—Matted together without Sheets or any thing else but only one Thread Bear blanket with double its Weight of Vermin such as Lice Fleas [etc.][2]

During the next three years, George's surveying jobs took him to the eastern edge of Virginia's frontier, into the Northern Neck and the Shenandoah Valley. George's efforts paid off. Eventually, he was able to earn enough money to buy his first piece of land—a lot on Bullskin Creek in Shenandoah. Owning land and slaves was the key to wealth in colonial Virginia. George would continue to buy property and slaves over the course of his lifetime.

George's Journal

George wrote about his experiences in the Ohio Valley. *The Journal of Major George Washington* was reprinted in colonial newspapers and as far away as Great Britain. George's journal described the environment in the Ohio Valley and provided readers with a sense of the large, open spaces.

Additionally, George described the people native to those lands. George did not reflect on his experiences but merely reported what he saw.

Washington learned how to survive in rugged country as a surveyor.

MILITARY MAN

In 1751, Lawrence planned a trip to Barbados. He had contracted tuberculosis and hoped the warmer climate would help cure him. Washington traveled with his half brother. The journey was his first ship voyage. It was also his first real exposure to military life, as Washington met military officers and visited Fort James in Barbados. While abroad, Washington came down with smallpox. He recovered, but the illness left small pockmarks on his face.

Upon his return home, Washington set his sights on a post in the Virginia militia. In 1752, he petitioned colonial Governor Robert Dinwiddie for an appointment. Lawrence was nearing death, and Washington wanted to inherit his half brother's military position. Young Washington had no experience as a soldier. Yet, he was confident and physically able, and he had the backing of the Fairfax family. Dinwiddie granted Washington the post. He became a major in the militia and headed out west. That same year, Lawrence died; his Mount Vernon estate would eventually pass on to Washington.

For the next five years, Washington participated in expeditions and learned many aspects of military

Dangerous Diseases

Tuberculosis is an infectious disease that can affect a person's lungs and other organs. Symptoms include weariness, coughing, fever, and weight loss. Today, treatments exist for this disease, but it was incurable during Washington's time and was usually fatal.

Smallpox is a disease that can cause skin rashes and high fevers. During Washington's time, it infected and killed many people. However, a person who survived the disease would develop immunity. Since the mid-twentieth century, smallpox has not infected anyone.

Pittsburgh, Pennsylvania

As Washington traveled through Ohio country, he noted the features of the land with an eye to later military defense. He reached the place where the Allegheny and the Monongahela rivers come together. He wrote, "I spent some time in viewing the Rivers, and the Land in this Fork, as it has the absolute Command of both Rivers. The Land at the Point is . . . very convenient for Building; the Rivers are each a Quarter of a Mile, or more, across, and run here very near at right Angles."[3] The area he described would soon become the site of the fought-over Fort Duquesne. Today, the area is the city of Pittsburgh, Pennsylvania.

life. He learned skills that would prove essential, as conflict was brewing on the western frontier. During the 1750s, two world powers laid claim to much of North America. The British occupied the Atlantic Coast, while the French claimed the land west of the Appalachian Mountains, including the Great Lakes and the Mississippi River Valley. However, the British disputed France's claim to the Ohio region west of the Appalachian Mountains.

By 1753, French activities in the Ohio country began to worry officials in Virginia. The colony of Virginia stretched west to border the large Ohio region, and many of Virginia's wealthy citizens had been granted land in Ohio by the British king. The French had moved troops south from Canada into the region and began building forts in areas that Britain also claimed. Governor Dinwiddie wrote to the British government about his concerns. In response, King George II ordered that a message be sent to the French, reasserting Britain's perceived rights over the territory.

The 21-year-old Washington was selected to head the important mission. He would deliver a message to the French on behalf of King George II. The message was very simple. It asserted Great Britain's rights and asked the French to leave the land the British considered theirs. Washington would travel to Fort Le Boeuf in the Ohio Valley, guided by an experienced fur trapper and trader, Christopher Gist. He also had an interpreter and several other men to help with their baggage, but no soldiers to protect them.

After a difficult journey, Washington arrived at Fort Le Boeuf. The French commander received Washington graciously. Still, he asserted that French claims to the territory were superior to those of the British. Washington had no choice but to return home with the news that the French would not surrender.

In Washington's journal of his travels, he described the heavy snow and freezing temperatures that he and Gist had to bear. He detailed the exhaustion of their horses, the raging rivers, and the difficult conditions. Washington told a story of an encounter with a small group of American Indians when the travelers were on their way home. The group ambushed the two travelers. One man shot at them from a short distance but missed, despite the close range. Gist and Washington caught the shooter and held him captive for a short time, but ultimately let the man go.

From among the local American Indian tribes, Washington befriended Seneca Chief Tanacharison, whom the British called "Half-King." The Seneca were one of six tribes that belonged to the powerful Iroquois Confederacy. Half-King represented the Iroquois nation's interests. In conflicts between the French and the British, Half-King usually supported the British. Washington was aware of the importance of allies. He appreciated the role the Seneca and other tribes could play in any conflict with the French. Washington's insight would prove accurate when the French and Indian War soon raged across the land. ⌐

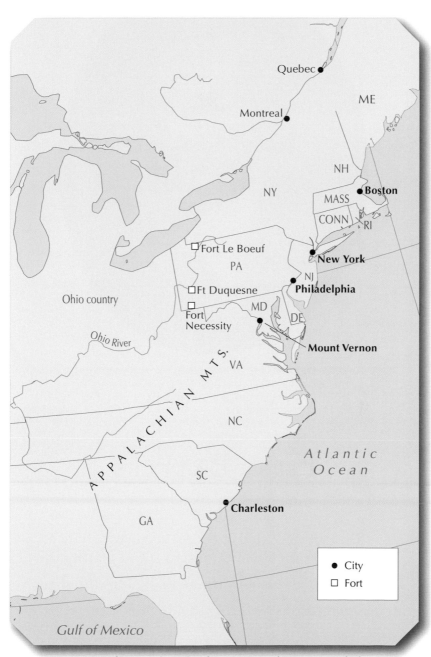

During the French and Indian War, Washington traveled from Virginia to several French forts in the Ohio region.

Washington served in the British military during the French and Indian War.

FIRST BATTLES

The French had no intention of leaving the land claimed by the British. They further increased tensions by trying to convince American Indian tribes to join in their cause. Some tribes sided with the French, while others supported the

British. The Virginia legislature, acting on behalf of the British government, decided that military action was needed. George Washington was appointed second in command of a regiment.

In April 1754, Washington set out ahead of his commander, Joshua Fry, with approximately 160 men. When they arrived in the Ohio Valley in May, Half-King provided Washington with information about the French and pledged his support to Washington's efforts. News came that the French had seized a British fort and had a strong military presence in the area. Fry had not arrived, which left Washington in charge.

Washington learned that some French troops were camped in the woods nearby. With a group of roughly 40 men, he separated from the main army to scout them out. With the help of Half-King and his warriors, Washington launched a surprise attack on the French troops on May 28. Ten Frenchmen were killed, including the commander, known as Jumonville.

During the clash, Jumonville had been wounded. After fighting had ceased, Half-King stepped forward and dealt the killing blow. Whatever Half-King's reasons for his action were, the Europeans

Washington leading his forces in an attack on the French

saw it as murder, not an act of war. The French
claimed that Washington's men and his Seneca allies
butchered a peaceful ambassador on a diplomatic
mission. Washington countered that the engagement
was warranted given the French threat. The incident
pushed the French and the British even closer
toward war.

FORT NECESSITY

Washington knew that the French were likely to counterattack. His scouting party rejoined his larger force in an area called Great Meadows. He needed a defensive position to protect them during battle. His men quickly built a round fort of logs with a ditch around it. They called it Fort Necessity. Washington's American Indian allies heard rumors of a huge French army headed their way and decided to leave. Washington and his men would have to face the French army alone.

British reinforcements arrived. Yet even with these additional soldiers, Washington's forces were outnumbered. With Jumonville's brother at the head, the French and their American Indian allies attacked on July 3. Washington's choice of location made his position dangerous. Rain filled the trenches in the fort, and Washington's men

Mixed Reactions

Washington wrote a letter home to one of his younger brothers that gave an account of the attack on Jumonville and the French soldiers. In his letter, he described his first taste of battle. He stated, "I heard Bullets whistle and believe me there was something charming in the Sound."[1] This quote was later published in Virginia's newspapers and was said to have been repeated in Great Britain. Some touted Washington as America's first war hero. Others thought he was bragging.

struggled to keep their gunpowder dry. Washington sent some men out of the fort into the meadow to try to lure the French into range of his guns. The French stayed in the trees, however, and their shots devastated the men outside the fort. The fort did not protect the men inside very well, either, and French bullets were getting through. Meanwhile, the French had good cover among the trees, making them difficult to hit. They surrounded the fort, trapping Washington and his men. Washington's troops began to lose hope, even more so after hearing rumors that many more American Indians were on their way to help the French.

In these unforgiving circumstances, Washington surrendered to the French.

Eighteenth-Century Warfare

In the eighteenth century, wars were fought with cannons, wooden sailing ships, horses, and muskets and bayonets. In most European battles, armies met across open fields and charged. Men on foot and on horseback rushed toward the enemy line, dodging bullets and cannonballs. Muskets could be fired only once before needing to be reloaded, so soldiers used bayonets or swords during the heat of battle. Muskets were also unreliable, inaccurate, and prone to misfiring.

Unlike the camouflage that soldiers often wear today, eighteenth-century uniforms were meant to stand out. In European fighting, it was important to see a soldier's uniform through the thick smoke of battle so as not to shoot friendly troops by accident. However, the British in North America soon found that their red uniforms made them easy targets in the forest.

His defeat was humiliating. He was forced to agree to terms of surrender in a document called the Articles of Capitulation. As the terms were in French, Washington had to rely on a translator to read them. The document allowed Washington and his men to leave Fort Necessity unharmed if they promised not to return to the Ohio country for one year. It also stated that Washington's troops had assassinated Jumonville, justifying the French attack. Washington later claimed that he had not understood the word *assassin.* He insisted that killing Jumonville had not been an act of murder. However, the French used this confession against the British as propaganda as the war continued.

MAJOR GENERAL EDWARD BRADDOCK

Washington had shown his inexperience as a soldier, and some people questioned his abilities. Washington resigned his post in 1754 and went to live at Mount Vernon, which he leased from his half brother's widow. However, Washington still saw his future in the military. When the opportunity arose in the spring of 1755, he volunteered to join the British forces fighting under Major General Edward Braddock. Braddock's mission was to remove the

French from the Ohio Valley, and he needed advice from someone who had experience in the region.

In May 1755, Washington joined Braddock's forces as an aide to the general. This provided him with the opportunity to spend time with British officers. Braddock soon recognized Washington's value and included him in military discussions.

Braddock led the way to the new French stronghold Fort Duquesne, at the forks of the Allegheny and Monongahela rivers. Travel through the wilderness of the Ohio country was difficult for the large group. With a segment of some 1,200 troops, Braddock moved ahead of the rest of the force. Washington wanted to join this advance troop, but he fell ill and was forced to stay back.

On July 8, Washington was still ill, but he was determined to join the advance party. He rode quickly to catch up with Braddock and his

Mother Washington

Washington's mother made it quite clear to her son that she did not want him in the military. Before Washington ultimately decided to join up with Major General Braddock's forces against the French, Washington's mother visited Mount Vernon. Mrs. Washington argued with her son, trying to influence him not to resume his military service. Washington seemed to have struggled with his decision for a time. Yet in the end, his own desires won out.

group. Soon, a large force of troops from Fort
Duquesne came upon Braddock's men and attacked
from the protective cover of the woods. Then the
British Redcoats made a fatal mistake: as was their
custom, they went into an open area and lined up in
formation to battle. Not only were they easy targets;
they could not see the enemy hiding behind rocks
and trees.

Braddock bravely rode into the center of
the fighting, where he was shot in the chest and
shoulder. Washington tried to rally the men. He
rode back and forth among the noise and smoke.
When his horse was shot out from under him, he
rode a different mount. That horse was killed as
well. In the midst of battle, four musket balls ripped
through Washington's uniform. Astonishingly, he
was not injured. By the end of the battle, Braddock's
forces had lost approximately 900 men. The French
and their American Indian allies suffered only 23
deaths. Braddock's forces retreated, but Braddock
did not survive the return trip.

Washington took note of what he had witnessed.
The experience of Braddock's expedition showed
him how conventional European fighting tactics
did not work in the wilderness of North America.

Rather, hiding in the woods and sneaking up on the enemy was most effective. He learned that a large force of soldiers also made a larger target for the enemy. A single large force should be separated and spread out. Perhaps most importantly, he observed firsthand how the British army could be defeated.

These observations taught Washington valuable strategies that he would later use during the Revolutionary War, although he still preferred to use conventional tactics when possible. ⌐

General Braddock was defeated on the way to Fort Duquesne.

Washington became commander in chief of Virginia's military.

COMMAND

Washington gained a reputation for his courage. He had rallied his men and organized the retreat of Braddock's soldiers. Word of his valor earned him a promotion in the Virginia regiment. The war between France and Britain

continued, but Washington's tasks mostly involved protecting settlers from American Indian attack.

Washington was 23 years old in the fall of 1755, when he became a colonel and the commander in chief of all Virginia forces. Washington gained military experience as he commanded what became a well-trained, effective, and disciplined force of men. He was a detail-oriented commander who took great pride in his men. Washington recognized the more successful woodland fighting tactics and trained his men to be more effective than Braddock's forces had been.

FORT DUQUESNE

The British were determined to take Fort Duquesne. In 1758, General John Forbes took the command. Recognizing Washington's experience and his soldiers' skills, Forbes added Washington and his troops to his larger force.

Forbes also listened to Washington's opinions on military matters. For example, Forbes accepted Washington's advice that

Professional Soldiers

Washington's militia was unlike the local militias that relied on volunteers. Washington's men were paid, professional fighters. He took great pride in their fighting skills. Yet Washington was frustrated that he and his colonial soldiers received less pay than British regulars. He tried to fight for pay equality, but his arguments fell on deaf ears.

the British regulars should not wear their well-recognized red coats. Instead, they wore uniforms that blended into the terrain. Moreover, Forbes had his soldiers trained in the kind of ambush warfare that Washington's men used.

Forbes included the Virginia regiment as part of his advance troop. Washington and the men he led arrived near Fort Duquesne in November. Forbes held a war council to determine the next steps. Mindful of Braddock's terrible defeat, the officers decided on a cautious approach.

The next day, the Virginia regiment came upon a group of enemy soldiers who were out on patrol. A battle quickly erupted. In the confusion, two sets of Washington's men began shooting at each other, believing that they were firing at the enemy. Washington quickly moved between the two groups. With great daring, he used his sword to push away the muskets of the men firing at each other.

Washington's troops suffered some casualties from the battle, but they also managed to capture three prisoners from Fort Duquesne. The prisoners revealed that the fort was not heavily guarded. Upon learning this intelligence, Forbes ordered an attack on the fort. But when Forbes and his troops arrived, they found the fort in flames. The French had fled. Despite this major victory, the French and Indian War continued until 1763. The French gave up most of their claims to land in North America. After a long and bloody war, the British triumphed.

BACK TO VIRGINIA

Washington had been living with his regiment for three years and was ready to establish his life in Virginia. He also wanted to marry a pleasant woman with money and a good reputation. He stood for election in the Virginia's governing body, the House of Burgesses, while he was still away on the Fort

The French and Indian War

War was fought between France and England from 1754 to 1763. The war began as a dispute over territory in North America, specifically in Ohio country, where both the French and British empires asserted claims. Tensions were already high when Washington attacked a French campsite on May 27, 1754. Other European powers quickly chose sides and became engulfed in the conflict. Known to Europeans as the Seven Years' War, the fighting eventually spread to many parts of the world where French and British interests were involved.

In North America, the French had more support from American Indian allies, but the British had a much larger colonial population than the French. The French had successes in battle at the beginning of the war. Toward the end, however, the British had better resources, larger naval forces, and more supplies. These advantages, along with improved tactics, allowed them to gain the upper hand.

The French economy was in trouble, and the country could no longer pay for the war. On February 10, 1763, the Treaty of Paris was signed. The French gave up most of their North American territories.

The British took Fort Duquesne in 1758.

Duquesne campaign. With the fort and the election won, Washington resigned from his military duty in December 1758 and returned to Virginia. Martha Dandridge Custis, a young widow, had caught his attention eight months previously, while he was home on sick leave. The two were possibly engaged before he left for Fort Duquesne. They were married after his return to Virginia, on January 6, 1759.

Martha was a wealthy woman who brought a large estate to the marriage. She also had two small children from her first marriage. Martha's children were four-year-old John, who was known as Jackie, and two-year-old Martha, who was known at Patsy. Together, this new family lived at Mount Vernon.

Washington was involved in his community as well. In addition to the Custis House of Burgesses, he held other local offices. He was in good standing in the community, not only because of his military exploits and political involvement, but also due to his marriage and status among wealthy Virginians. Washington worked hard, managed the details of his estate, and acquired vast amounts of land. He became a very wealthy man.

Stepchildren

When Washington married Martha Dandridge Custis, he became stepfather to her two children from her first marriage, Jackie and Patsy. Patsy suffered from seizures and epileptic fits during her life. She died at the age of 17 in 1773. Jackie fell ill with a camp fever and died in 1781. George was by Jackie's side when he died. George and Martha did not have any children together.

KING GEORGE III

While Washington focused on being a Virginia farmer, Great Britain was facing changes. In 1760, King George II had died. His grandson George III took the throne next. Additionally, the British Parliament in London, England, was grappling with massive debts from the French and Indian war. Britain needed its colonies to contribute. After all, many British believed it was only right

Washington's Estate

Mount Vernon provided all the needs of those who lived there. It included a mill, a schooner (to catch fish from the nearby Potomac River), a smoke-house, a dairy, a cloth factory, orchards, and crops such as tobacco, corn, and wheat.

Indentured white servants worked on the estate, but most of the workers were slaves. At one point, Washington owned as many as 200 slaves.

that the colonists help pay for their protection from the French.

Parliament passed the Stamp Act in 1765. The Stamp Act applied to printed items including magazines, newspapers, and other documents. The buyer had to buy a stamp that showed the tax had been paid. The colonists strongly objected to these taxes. They opposed "taxation without representation"—although they were taxed, the colonists had no elected officials in Parliament.

Colonies sent petitions to London protesting the taxes. Some colonists suggested that a boycott of British goods would be more effective. When London merchants suffered from the boycott, Parliament paid attention. The Stamp Act was repealed in 1766. However, the government continued to impose new taxes on all sorts of goods.

Washington was a man of action, but he was a good judge of circumstances and people. Washington agreed with the colonists and supported these boycotts, but it would be three more years before he would become a leader in the growing conflict.

Washington married Martha Dandridge Custis, a widow with two young children.

*Patrick Henry urged the House of Burgesses
to take action against the British.*

TAXATION WITHOUT
REPRESENTATION

*I*n 1767, the British passed the Townshend
Act. This set a tax on items such as tea,
paint, glass, and paper. Colonists considered this
more taxation without representation. Patrick Henry
of Virginia asserted that only the colonists had the

right to tax themselves. People began to question the relationship between Britain and its colonies.

On May 18, 1769, Washington became a leader for the first time in the growing movement. At the time, the cities of Boston, New York, and Philadelphia were boycotting British goods. He urged Virginians to do the same. Washington also followed the boycott himself. Ultimately, the boycott worked. Parliament felt compelled to repeal most of the hated taxes. However, the ruling body did not repeal its tax on tea. The colonists still felt the British government's control over them.

In 1768, the British crown sent troops to Boston to control the increasingly unruly city. Tensions erupted between the military and civilians on the night of March 5, 1770. A mob taunted a group of soldiers, who opened fire on the crowd. The five who died in what became known as the Boston Massacre were the first casualties of the impending crisis.

Tea and a Tempest

The colonists avoided the tax on tea by buying illegal imports from other countries. The British Parliament responded in May 1773 when it passed the Tea Act. This reduced the tax on the British–

owned East India Company tea and allowed the company to sell directly to consumers. However, the act had the potential to put colonial merchants out of business. The act pushed middle class and wealthy colonists who may have previously been on the British side to join their protesting countrymen.

Sons of Liberty

When the colonists began objecting to the British government's taxes, many would not speak publicly for fear of retaliation. Some men assembled in secret clubs where they could discuss their opinions and objections freely.

The Sons of Liberty was one of these groups, and Samuel Adams was one of its leaders. He was an agitator who had the ability to stir others to action. Adams served as a delegate to both Continental Congresses. He was also one of the 56 men who would sign the Declaration of Independence in 1776. Years later, he served as governor of Massachusetts.

It made others mad as well. Many colonists believed the lower prices on East India Company tea were a trick. If they bought the tea, they would be paying Parliament's taxes. They did not want Parliament to say that they were accepting the tax because they bought the tea.

Some merchants sent their tea back to Britain. More tea sat in warehouses as people refused to buy it. Soon, a group called the Sons of Liberty organized a visible and daring protest known today as the Boston Tea Party.

On December 16, 1773, members of the Sons of Liberty staged a protest. A group dressed themselves as members of the Mohawk tribe.

Protestors dumped tea into Boston Harbor during the Boston Tea Party.

They climbed aboard three British ships in Boston's harbor and pitched chests of tea into the sea. None of the other cargo on the ships was disturbed. The protestors sent the British government the message that they would not put up with unfair taxes.

The British government responded with a loud and clear answer. Parliament passed more laws to punish the colonies. The colonists referred to these as the Intolerable Acts. In Massachusetts, a British officer took control of the government and closed Boston's port, stopping trade in the city.

ESCALATION

Parliament's repressive actions in Massachusetts caused colonists everywhere to rally against Great Britain. Washington was among those who supported the cause. He believed that Great Britain was abusing the people of Boston. In the spring of 1774, the governing bodies of each colony except Georgia chose representatives to meet and discuss the British problem. The Virginia assembly selected Washington, Patrick Henry, and others to attend the meeting.

In September 1774, 56 delegates from 12 colonies met at the First Continental Congress in Philadelphia. Despite their different backgrounds and opinions, the delegates agreed

Patrick Henry

Patrick Henry is one of the most famous leaders of the American Revolution. A great orator, he believed strongly in the idea that people have inherent, inalienable rights. Henry spoke out against British taxation without representation. When he argued against the hated Stamp Act, he declared that the colonies had the right to make their own laws, independent of Great Britain.

Among many other roles, Henry was a delegate to the Continental Congress with George Washington in 1774 and then again in 1775. On March 23, 1775, he gave his famous speech, saying, "I know not what course others may take; but as for me, give me liberty or give me death!"[1] Henry stated these famous words in St. John's Church in Richmond, Virginia, at the second Virginia Convention. He was reaching the conclusion that war with England was unavoidable, as were many other colonists.

that the colonists had basic rights. Specifically, they focused on the rights to life, liberty, and property. The delegates denounced the British oppression in Boston and the presence of British troops in America. Most wanted a peaceful resolution. After much discussion, members of the Continental Congress ended trade with Great Britain.

In the colonies, local militias were training for conflict. Washington helped organize Virginia's military preparations. In April 1775, British troops and Patriot militias clashed at the towns of Lexington and Concord in Massachusetts. The Revolutionary War had begun.

The Continental Army

In May, Washington went to the Second Continental Congress in Philadelphia. Washington wore his military uniform to the meetings. Some scholars say that he was showing support for the cause. Others believe that Washington wanted to be commander of the colonial forces. Whatever his motives, Washington made a good impression. John Adams noted, "Colonel Washington appears at Congress in his uniform and by his great experiences and abilities in military matters, is of much service to us."[2] Adams nominated Washington as the army's commander in chief. The decision was unanimous: Washington was chosen to lead the fight against the British.

Washington accepted, but he added:

I beg it may be remembered by every Gentleman in the room, that I this day declare with the utmost sincerity, I do not think my self equal to the Command I am honoured with.[3]

Leading the Army

Volunteers from New England made up much of the troops in the first months of the war. At the time, members of different colonies felt little national unity and were citizens of their own colonies first. And yet, the Continental Congress chose Washington, a Virginian, to lead a group from New England.

John Adams believed putting a southerner in command of northerners would help unite the colonies. Washington was a hero of the French and Indian War. He also had invaluable leadership skills. He proved to be the right leader for the job.

The new commander in chief of the Continental army had not fought in 16 years. Nor had he ever led an army unit larger than a regiment. His army was new and untested. The British officers he would face in battle doubtless had much more military experience. The enemy's army and navy were the most powerful in the world. How could this farmer from Virginia possibly lead his troops to victory? As more British ships set course for the colonies, Washington was about to find out.

Washington took command of the Continental army in 1775.

Boston as seen from Dorchester Heights in 1774

COMMANDER IN CHIEF

On June 17, 1775, New England militia units were entrenched on Breed's Hill in Boston. They were attacked by British troops in what became one of the first major battles of the Revolutionary War. The British overwhelmed the

Patriot force, but at a cost of 1,000 British soldiers—roughly half of their forces. In contrast, the Patriots had few casualties. Both sides claimed victory after the Battle of Breed's Hill, which was later known as the Battle of Bunker Hill. The British had the hill, but the Patriots had made them pay dearly for it. Untrained civilians fighting for freedom had stood up against the professional soldiers of the great British army.

On July 3, 1775, Washington took command of 16,000 militiamen outside of Boston in what became known as the siege of Boston. Washington had suffered his humiliating defeat at Fort Necessity exactly 21 years before. In the coming months and years, Washington would again face many challenges. His soldiers were farmers who had left their fields or townsmen who had left their businesses. His army had little money, so the men had poor uniforms and very little gunpowder. Despite Washington's attempts to keep the camps clean, many fell ill and disease was widespread. Some men began to desert the army almost as soon as they arrived. Militiamen usually signed up to serve for only one year, so the army was consistently in need of new recruits. Instead of trained and seasoned veterans, Washington was constantly dealing with new, untried men. On top of everything else, men from New England were not inclined to trust men from the south, or vice versa, so regiments from different colonies did not want to cooperate.

Some still hoped for peace with Great Britain. But King George III's speech at the opening of Parliament in October destroyed that chance. The king charged the colonists with rebellion and was determined to make them obey. There would be no compromise nor any consideration of the colonists' appeals. Military force was the king's only approach. Soon, many colonists began to call for independence. Published in January 1776, Thomas Paine's pamphlet *Common Sense* laid out the case for independence and was widely read throughout the colonies.

Then, in March 1776, Washington's actions changed the course of the war. With the utmost

Olive Branch Petition

In July 1775, despite the battles that had already occurred, some colonists still hoped for a peaceful solution with Great Britain. The Continental Congress wrote and signed a message, now called the Olive Branch Petition, and sent it to the king. In it, the colonists told the king that they wanted to be loyal subjects. They blamed the conflict on Parliament and asked the king to intervene on their behalf. However, the king rejected the petition. The colonists then knew they would have to fight for their freedoms.

secrecy, Washington and his men crafted a daring plan. Under the cover of darkness on the night of March 4, Washington sent men up to Dorchester Heights, an area overlooking Boston and its harbor. Through the night, the men quickly built fortifications. On the next day, the anniversary of the Boston Massacre, Washington asked his men to "remember it is the fifth of March, and avenge the death of your brethren."[1]

The British were shocked to find cannons pointing down at them from Dorchester Heights. Realizing the great danger they were in, the British saw no choice but to load

Council of War

Washington made up his own mind about military decisions, but he also considered the advice of a council of war. At times, he accepted the council's judgment, even if he was inclined to take another course.

In Boston, members of his council of war included three major generals and four brigadier generals. Major General Charles Lee was one of the only professional soldiers of the group. Lee was Washington's second in command and a fellow southerner. Like Washington, Lee had served in the British army during the French and Indian War and had fought in the Braddock campaign. The Mohawk people called Lee "Boiling Water" because of his hot temper. Washington thought that Lee was "the first officer in military knowledge and experience we have in the whole army."[2]

Other members of the war council included Major General Artemus Ward, a veteran of the French and Indian War; John Thomas of Massachusetts, a physician; William Heath of Massachusetts, a farmer; John Sullivan of New Hampshire, a lawyer and politician; and Nathanael Greene of Rhode Island.

their ships and sail away, yielding the city to Washington and his men.

Success

News of the Continental army's spectacular victory, Washington's brilliance, and Britain's humiliation traveled throughout the colonies. It was now the spring of 1776, and the colonists had not yet declared independence from Great Britain. New York City and the Hudson River were under the greatest threat from the British. The Continental Congress asked Washington to make every effort to defend New York.

Washington selected General Charles Lee, a man considered to be an expert in military matters, to defend New York. Lee went ahead, and Washington followed later in spring 1776. In June, Washington established forces on Long Island and Manhattan. The British took positions on Staten Island,

Loyalists

Outside of Boston, the Continental army laid siege. Inside Boston, British soldiers resided along with many colonists who remained loyal to the king. These loyal British subjects, also known as Tories, had taken refuge in the city. The British military and the Loyalists in Boston used disdainful names such as "the rebels" or "rabble in arms"[3] to refer to Washington's army. The Patriots had a few names for the British as well, calling them "lobsterbacks" because of their red coats.[4]

where many Loyalists, or colonists sympathetic to the British, lived. Both sides recognized that in New York City, command of the waterways could mean victory or defeat.

CLAIMING INDEPENDENCE

On July 2, 1776, delegates to the Continental Congress in Philadelphia moved to "dissolve the connection" with Great Britain.[5] On July 4, they approved the Declaration of Independence. This momentous declaration was legally an act of treason against the British. If the Patriots lost the war, the delegates could be imprisoned or executed. The course was set, and a new phase in the war had begun.

Washington's men cheered at the news. The general himself viewed the Declaration of Independence as a "fresh incentive to every officer and soldier to act with fidelity and courage."[6] Washington recognized

Edmund Burke

Not all in Parliament agreed with the decision to go to war with the colonists. Some British lawmakers, such as Edmund Burke, admired the Patriots for their principled stance. On one occasion, Burke stood in Parliament for two and one-half hours arguing against going to war. Burke pleaded to "keep the poor, giddy, thoughtless people of our country from plunging headlong into this impious war."[7]

that, despite the recent success, the British were still determined to quash the rebellion. A massive British fleet was crossing the Atlantic. Alarm guns were about to sound in New York. ⁓

The Declaration of Independence was signed in Philadelphia on July 4, 1776.

The Continental army was in constant need of new recruits.

ATTACK ON NEW YORK

The Continental army had established fortifications in and around New York City. Although Washington's total army numbered approximately 19,000 men, they were separated in smaller groups around the New York area. Discipline was poor, and many of the troops were new to fighting. More and more British ships—the largest force Great Britain had ever sent forth—sailed into New York waters carrying British officers, troops, equipment, and supplies. Some estimate the total British force by mid-August 1776 at more than 30,000 troops. The odds were stacked against the Patriot cause.

THE BATTLE OF BROOKLYN

An army of 10,000 Patriots guarded Brooklyn Heights on Long Island. Washington was in Manhattan with most of the rest of his forces. The British troops began landing on Long Island on the beaches to the south of the Continental forces on August 22. Washington's divided forces were not in good communication, so only part of the army was aware of the British movements. In addition, the Patriot commander on Long Island was unfamiliar with the area. He did not know where it was most important

A Difficult Situation

Some historians believe that Washington's situation in New York was precarious from the start. He had no navy but was surrounded by water. Some argue that given these circumstances, Washington had no way to succeed whether the British attacked Manhattan or Long Island. General Lee had clearly stated to Washington that "whoever commands the sea must command the town."[1] Events proved Lee's assessment correct.

to send scouts or which roads he needed to defend. Their defense left holes that the British would find and exploit.

On the night of August 26, a large British force made an unexpected move. Finding an unguarded road, it maneuvered around the Continental army under cover of darkness. At dawn, the troops would be able to attack from the north. More British troops were poised to attack from the south. With them were hired soldiers from Germany known as Hessians.

Early in the morning on August 27, British cannons boomed and muskets blasted. The Continental army was surprised by the onslaught. In the midst of the panic and confusion, many Patriot soldiers fought

Peace Talks

Before the battles at New York began, General William Howe, the British commander, made an overture for peace through his emissaries. Washington did not believe that the British were acting in good faith. Still, he went through the motions of a very formal interview with British Colonel James Patterson.

On July 20, 1776, Colonel Patterson met Washington in New York City. Washington's guard stood at attention as Washington received Patterson with civility and formality. Patterson tried to flatter Washington and stated that the king wanted to end the dispute. Washington responded by saying that he was not given the authority to end the hostilities. Washington also told General Howe that he wished no pardon from the British. He said, "those who have committed no fault want no pardon. We are only defending what we deem our indisputable rights."[2]

back bravely. Washington came from Manhattan with reinforcements, but it was no use. The British attack had been perfectly timed and choreographed. The Patriots suffered terrible losses, and many were taken prisoner. Despite all attempts to prepare for the British, Washington's army was devastated at the Battle of Brooklyn, later called the Battle of Long Island. As they retrenched behind their fortifications at Brooklyn Heights on August 28, the Continental forces had only three options: fight and lose against a far superior force, retreat, or surrender.

The Patriots were lucky that the British General William Howe did not decide to continue the attack, or the cause might have been lost. Instead, the British circled the Patriots and began preparing for a siege. Continental forces inside the Brooklyn fort were trapped. Their only possible escape route was over the East River to Manhattan. But the winds had to blow in the right direction for the escape to work, and British warships were a dangerous threat. Washington needed information. Brigadier General Thomas Mifflin volunteered

The Brave Marylanders

As the battle raged in Brooklyn, Washington knew that the situation was desperate. In particular, the troops from Maryland, led by William Alexander, pushed back the enemy again and again. It is said that Washington watched those men battle for their lives and cried out, "Good God, what brave fellows I must this day lose!"[3]

to assess the Continental army's outer defenses and report his findings to Washington.

The skies grew dark and a storm raged, making conditions even worse for Washington's troops. Food was scarce, there was little shelter from the rain, and the men struggled to keep their muskets and gunpowder dry. Washington wrote a brief letter to Congress reporting on the stressful situation. But with little information from the field, he had few options.

Although he was running on little sleep, Washington remained calm. He rode on horseback to visit his men and offered words of encouragement. Washington learned from General Mifflin that the enemy was approaching. He sent a secret message to General William Heath at the East River, ordering him to gather every boat he could find. Concealed by darkness and fog, the Continental army silently began

Nathanael Greene and the Battle of Brooklyn

Washington had great faith in the judgment and skills of General Nathanael Greene and put him in command of Long Island. Greene worked furiously to prepare for a British attack on the strategically important location.

Greene fell terribly ill before the Battle of Brooklyn. Washington was forced to replace him with what he felt was an inferior commander. The new commander was not familiar with the area and showed poor judgment by not setting out enough sentries. Washington believed that the battle might have had a different outcome if Greene had not become sick.

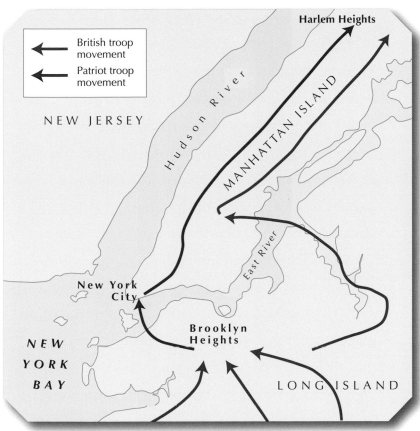

Troop movement on Long Island and Manhattan Island, 1776

its retreat at night on August 29. The rain ceased, but the winds delayed the river crossing. Then, suddenly, the wind changed. Boats carried soldiers, horses, cannons, and supplies across the river. With men rowing hour after hour, the boats made trip after trip across the river.

Washington rode to the river to watch his men cross. Mifflin and his troops had the most dangerous assignment of protecting the soldiers at the back while the rest of the Patriot troops departed. Washington's men worked feverishly, desperate to escape before the British discovered them. But dawn was approaching on August 30, and they would not be able to hide under cover of darkness any longer. To their good fortune, shortly after daybreak, a dense fog rolled in. It completely hid the Patriot's actions from British sight.

Finally, Mifflin and his men were called to the boats. Washington remained on the bank until the last of his troops had departed safely; then he, too, crossed the river. Withdrawing an army under normal circumstances was challenging enough, yet Washington had secretly moved 9,000 troops across the river in one night. It was a bold, well-executed maneuver.

When the British realized what had happened, they were astonished. Although the British claimed a resounding victory, they had not wiped out Washington's army. Instead, they had allowed Washington and his troops to survive to continue the fight. —

Washington retreated from Brooklyn under the cover of darkness and fog.

William Howe commanded the British army from 1775 to 1778.

A DEFENSIVE WAR

Aside from the well-executed escape, the exhausted Continental army had little to celebrate. Washington and his men were safe in New York City, but the British remained perilously close by. Several of Washington's officers believed that they should withdraw further. Without holding Long Island, they reasoned, they could not defend New York City. Congress agreed, and Washington began the evacuation in early September, heading to the northern part of the city.

Washington was at his command position in the northern part of the city when the British attacked on September 15, 1776. As cannons boomed and guns blazed, the city's remaining residents fled in terror. Hearing the ferocious assault, Washington rode toward the battle. He galloped his horse into fleeing soldiers. He tried to rally them to fight, but they were too panicked. The British were at their heels. Washington rode dangerously close to the firing enemy, but he did not suffer any injury. Two of his aides grabbed the bridle of his horse and hustled him to safety. Fortunately for Washington and his men, the British halted their assault as they waited for the rest of their force.

Captain Nathan Hale

Captain Nathan Hale, a 21-year-old man from Connecticut, volunteered to collect desperately needed information for Washington. He was caught by the British in New York and ultimately confessed that he was a spy. Without the benefit of a trial, he was promptly hanged. Reports said that as Hale was about to be hanged, his last words spoken were, "I only regret that I have but one life to give for my country."[1] Hale's fate and his last words became part of the lore of the American Revolution.

Washington and his men retreated to the northern part of the city at Harlem Heights. On September 16, a small scouting mission of 100 Continental troops encountered a British group with approximately four times as many soldiers. A battle erupted. The fight escalated as both sides sent in reinforcements, but the Patriots gained the upper hand. The Continental army claimed the battle of Harlem Heights as a much-needed win. The minor victory lifted the soldiers' morale. Meanwhile, the rest of the Patriot army completed its withdrawal. As the British took over the city, Continental forces camped on the high ground above the Harlem River, a secure vantage point.

Mrs. Murray

After the battles of New York, a fable spread of a woman named Mrs. Robert Murray, who was devoted to the Patriot cause. Legend has it that Mrs. Murray slowed down the advancing British by inviting General Howe and his men to join her for tea and wine. While Howe and his troops enjoyed her offer, the Patriots were able to escape.

Escape from New York

The situation was dire, compelling the Patriots to withdraw further north. They stationed almost 3,000 men to hold Fort Washington, north of Harlem at the top of Manhattan Island. As the rest of the army retreated on October 17, the British advanced. On October 18, Patriot soldiers attacked the advancing British. The Continental army's fierce fighting and tenacity surprised the British. The British advance was disrupted, and they now proceeded with more caution.

However, the British had obtained key information. Continental soldiers who had turned traitor briefed the British on the Patriots' defenses. Additionally, some of Washington's letters containing secret information had been intercepted. The British attacked Fort Washington on November 16. There were too few soldiers to defend the fort, and it easily fell. It was another crushing blow for the Patriots.

Washington had faced one disastrous, humiliating loss after another in New York. Many, including members of Congress, criticized Washington and his officers for mistakes in judgment. The Continental army received word

Molly the Hero

The surrender of Fort Washington was a terrible blow to the Continental army. There were few Patriot heroes to celebrate after that awful loss. One person who stood out for her uncommon bravery during that combat was Margaret "Molly" Corbin. Her husband was a Pennsylvania soldier named John Corbin. When John fell, Molly took his place in battle, loading and firing a cannon at the enemy. Molly was hurt during the fighting and almost lost her arm. When the Continental army surrendered, the British allowed Molly to go back to Pennsylvania.

that the British would next attack Fort Lee, directly across the Hudson River from Fort Washington. Washington ordered a quick evacuation of the fort at the end of November. Huge amounts of ammunition and arms fell into British hands, another big loss for the Continental army.

PENNSYLVANIA

Washington struggled with a disorderly army that kept losing men to sickness and desertion. As Washington and his army retreated through New Jersey, they faced terrible conditions. Many soldiers were without shelter, shoes, or food.

Washington was concerned for his men's health and welfare. He also worried as the end of his men's enlistment periods neared, and the states were unwilling to send more soldiers. Many, including his own officers, lost faith in him, and many soldiers deserted. General Charles Lee refused to send his force of 3,000, perhaps hoping that Washington would fail and he would become commander in his place.

Popular support for the war also greatly diminished. The British believed that victory was near. Reports of British looting, plundering, and brutality spread. The fall and winter of 1776 were a very difficult time for the American Revolution and Washington.

As winter worsened, the situation became even more desperate. Yet Washington did not despair. He trusted in his loyal generals more than ever. Some noted that adversity seemed only to increase Washington's energy. Washington decided that he needed to make a bold stroke, one that would inflict damage on the enemy and rally the Patriots.

General Charles Lee

General Charles Lee had served in the British army and was one of the most experienced officers in the Continental army. His reputation was only enhanced by his successes in South Carolina against the British during the summer of 1776. However, Lee did not respect the decisions of the Continental Congress. In addition, he thought that he could do a better job than Washington and wanted command of the army.

After the loss of Fort Lee in November 1776, Washington called Lee and his troops north from South Carolina to help Patriot efforts in New Jersey. But Lee refused to rejoin the main army. Some historians speculate that Lee wanted Washington to fail so that Lee would take over command.

Washington called for Lee and his troops again in December. This time, Lee did not refuse outright. However, Lee moved slowly and kept coming up with excuses. On December 12, 1776, Lee spent the night in a tavern with only a personal guard of 15 officers and soldiers. A Loyalist gave the British Lee's position, and the next morning the tavern was surrounded by British cavalry. Still in his dressing gown, Lee was taken away. He was held captive by the British until he was ransomed in the spring of 1778, when he became second-in-command again.

Washington surprised the Hessians at Trenton when he crossed the Delaware River in a snowstorm.

A Daring Stroke

General Howe decided to suspend the British campaign for the winter months and retire to the safety and comfort of New York City. He stationed soldiers in a series of locations around New Jersey. A group of approximately 1,500 Hessian soldiers from Germany were stationed in Trenton, New Jersey. They camped across the Delaware River from Washington's force on the Pennsylvania side. Philadelphia, Pennsylvania, where the Continental Congress met, was only a day's march away from the British army.

On Christmas Day 1776, Washington staged a daring attack on the outpost in Trenton. He would not confront the better-equipped and better-trained enemy in a traditional battle. Instead, he would attack in stealth as was done so successfully in the French and Indian War. It was practically unheard of for European armies to attack in the winter. The attack was doubly a surprise because Christmas was usually considered to be a time of truce. Around midnight, Washington's troops crossed the icy and dangerous Delaware River on boats. The Germans were taken completely by surprise the morning of December 26 and surrendered. In the attack, 21 Hessians were killed in combat, 90 were wounded, and 900 were taken prisoner. Only four men in the Continental army were wounded. Not a single Patriot soldier died in combat that day. The battle of Trenton was a masterful stroke by Washington, reinvigorating his men and improving public opinion.

British officer General Charles Cornwallis was sent with 5,500 troops to strike back at Washington. After they marched to Trenton, they set camp for the night across a small river from Washington's forces. Just after midnight on the morning of January 3,

Johann Gottlieb Rall

Johann Gottlieb Rall had fought with the British at Fort Washington and other battles. For his bravery, he was given command at Trenton and took charge of the Hessian soldiers. Rall received warnings that the Continental army would attack. Even so, Rall did not expect an attack in the middle of the night during a winter storm. Caught unprepared, Rall was mortally wounded, and his forces surrendered.

1777, Washington quietly and secretly withdrew his men. He had left men behind at camp to maintain the fires and keep up the impression of a camped army. The British did not suspect anything until after Washington and his men were gone. Washington slipped around the bulk of the British army and surprised the smaller force that had been left to guard the town of Princeton. Taking the Princeton guard by surprise, Washington won his second battle in just over a week.

Unable to hold Princeton against the main force of the British army, however, Washington and his men pulled back to a winter camp in Morristown, New Jersey. Already, 1777 was looking brighter for Washington and his soldiers.

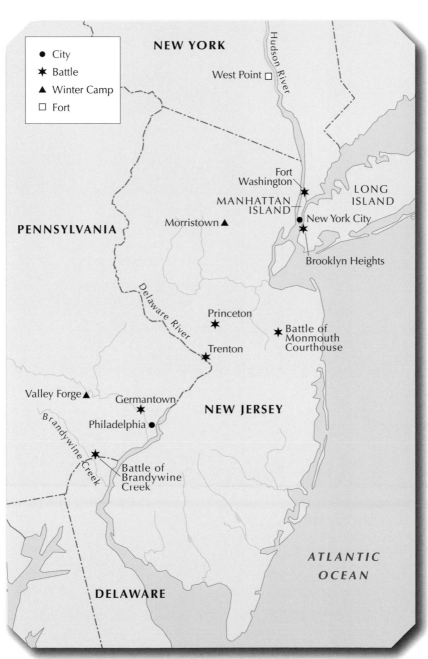

Washington's New York, New Jersey, and Pennsylvania battlefields

The Battle of Brandywine Creek allowed the British to take Philadelphia.

THE ARMY SURVIVES

Washington was invigorated by his recent success, and his army was inspired to continue the fight. The hungry and cold men made it through the winter, and the French sent supplies to keep the army on its feet. During spring 1777, most of the fighting took place in the northern part of the colony of New York. Washington and his men in New Jersey saw little action until later in the year.

The British wanted to capture the colonial government in Philadelphia. British General Howe led an attack on Washington's men near the city on September 11, 1777. Washington and his men fought hard at the Battle of Brandywine Creek. However, Howe outmaneuvered Washington and his commanders, and the Patriots sustained many losses. Washington retreated, and the Continental Congress fled Philadelphia. On September 26, General Howe and his British forces invaded the city of Philadelphia itself. Washington regrouped, and early in the morning on October 4, he led an assault on the British at Germantown, Pennsylvania. This was the first time that Washington had led an attack against the main British force. In previous battles, Washington had been defending or he had attacked smaller British detachments.

The assault was intended to be a surprise, but Loyalists had warned Howe shortly before it began. Even so, matters looked good for the Continental army until a thick fog rolled in. Utterly confused, one part of the army attacked other Patriots, mistaking them for the British. The Continental forces missed a perfect opportunity to press their attack and instead retreated from the field. The British and Continental forces suffered similar numbers of dead and wounded, between 500 and 600 each, but the British took an additional 400 Patriots prisoner. The British held the battlefield.

"I Shall Quit the Helm"

Some critics went so far as to suggest removing Washington from power. At one point, a political campaign was underway to undermine Washington's command of the army. Washington kept a cool head and did not become embroiled in politics. Instead, he simply let it be known that "Whenever the public gets dissatisfied with my services, or a person is found better qualified to answer her expectations, I shall quit the helm."[1] Once the possibility of Washington stepping down seemed real, all challenges to his authority died.

Europe Takes Note

General John Burgoyne commanded the British forces in the north, which had marched south from Canada to fight the Patriots during the spring of 1777. As Washington led his troops in Pennsylvania, General Horatio Gates led another part of the Continental army north in Albany, New York. Gates was supported by militias from New England, and Washington sent Gates an experienced general named Benedict Arnold.

On October 17, the Patriots defeated the British in the Battle of Saratoga, New York. Benedict

Arnold was a hero. Word of the Continental army's success spread as far as Europe, damaging the British reputation of military superiority. Support for the war in Britain wavered, and the French took note of the Patriot victories. In February 1778, the French would sign a formal alliance with the colonies.

Washington continued to lead a defensive war. He would keep his army together and cause as much trouble as possible for the British army without meeting them in full battle. Ignoring his critics, he accepted the fact that this would not be a swift victory. On December 17, 1777, Washington ordered his men to Valley Forge, Pennsylvania, to settle in for the winter. Exhausted and starving, they survived winter in makeshift log huts. Washington described these conditions:

> To see Men without Cloathes to cover their nakedness, without Blankets to lay on, without Shoes, by which their Marches might be traced by the Blood from their feet, is a mark of Patience and obedience which in my opinion can scarce be paralel'd.[2]

Foreign Policy

Washington had a keen sense of the realities and limitations of alliances with foreign nations. In a letter on November 14, 1778, regarding the alliance with France, Washington wrote, "No nation is to be trusted farther than it is bound by its interest; and no prudent statesman or politician will venture to depart from it."[3]

The Continental army barely survived the winter of
1777–1778 at Valley Forge.

Resources were not coming in, and public
enthusiasm for the war continued to shrink. Few
state governments would tax their residents or force
men to enlist. Thus, the Continental Congress
could not supply money or additional troops to
Washington.

Washington wrote a letter to Henry Laurens,
president of the Continental Congress:

*I am now convinced beyond a doubt that unless some great
and capital change suddenly takes place in that line, this
Army must inevitably be reduced to one or other of these three
things. Starve—dissolve—or disperse.*[4]

THE WAR DRAGS ON

Washington lost countless men to disease and the harsh conditions at Valley Forge. Yet through the winter and spring, the Continental army welcomed new recruits, and many men reenlisted. Many of those men would serve Washington until the end of the war. The Prussian Friedrich Steuben, who called himself Baron von Steuben, joined the Patriots. His experience in leading practice drills greatly improved the army's battle skills. In May 1778, Washington marched his men out of Valley Forge. He also received the welcome news that the French had joined the war on the side of the Patriots. In May, the Continental Congress also promised bonuses for all men serving for the duration of the war.

Since he had failed to stop the rebellion, General Howe resigned. Sir Henry Clinton became the new commander for the British. He ordered the British force in Philadelphia to depart for New York City. In June, Washington had advance notice that the British were going to leave their fortifications. He organized a plan of attack on Clinton's troops, including a French volunteer, the Marquis de Lafayette, as commander. Lafayette was Washington's student in military command, and the general treated Lafayette almost as a son. However, Major General Charles Lee opposed the mission. If the mission were to proceed, he demanded to be put in charge. Washington gave in to Lee's request. Lee led the troops in what later became known as the Battle at Monmouth Court House. Lee's attack failed, and he ordered a retreat. Washington considered Lee's actions disgraceful and took away his command.

Washington took over. As he rallied the soldiers, his forces gained the upper hand. However, the Patriots could not destroy the British army, and Clinton's soldiers retreated to safety in New York City.

The war dragged on. Clinton was holed up in New York. Washington and his troops

General Howe's Loss

General William Howe took over command of the British army in 1775 and led the British to victories in New York in 1776. Howe had served in the French and Indian War, and he knew how to use and defend against the guerrilla tactics used in that war.

However, several factors contributed to his removal from command in 1778. He had several opportunities, especially in New Jersey and Philadelphia in late 1776 and 1777, when he could have overwhelmed Washington's force and ended the war. However, Howe had moved too slowly, allowing Washington to retreat and fight another day. After the Battle of Brandywine in September 1777, Howe could have chosen to chase and crush the Continentals, but he instead settled into Philadelphia. He was reluctant to fight during the winter, giving Washington time to regroup and recruit. Worst of all, his inability to coordinate with General Burgoyne in New York contributed to Burgoyne's total defeat.

survived another unforgiving winter of blizzards and storms in Morristown, New Jersey. Washington hoped that French support would be an advantage, but the French ships were protecting their interests in the Caribbean instead of attacking the British in North America. Washington recognized that the French were only involved in the war as long as it served their own purposes.

As his men suffered under deplorable conditions, Washington argued that he needed more support for his army. He came to the conclusion that the effectiveness of Congress was limited by its lack of authority. In 1780, he publicly stated his belief that the colonies needed a more powerful central government.

A Traitor Within

In August 1780, Washington placed military hero Benedict Arnold in charge of the fort at West Point, New York. Washington considered West Point important because it guarded the Hudson River. Arnold tried to turn the fort over to the British in exchange for 20,000 pounds, equivalent to millions of dollars today. His treachery was exposed when his British contact was captured by the Patriots and found carrying Arnold's letters to the British. Benedict Arnold fled on a British ship, leaving his British contact to be hanged as a spy. This betrayal was a terrible blow to Washington and made him wonder whom he could trust. For his part, Arnold earned himself the hostility of both sides, but he was made a British brigadier general.

While Washington remained in New York, the British campaign moved south. Washington sent a force with General Horatio Gates south to fight, but the British attained major victories at Charleston, South Carolina; Savannah, Georgia; and Camden, South Carolina.

Revolt

Through 1780 and 1781, Washington's army fought no significant battles. When money and food ran low in January 1781, a group of soldiers even revolted and took over Princeton, New Jersey. Officers had to promise the men extra pay to get them to rejoin the army. Washington believed he would have less trouble with discipline if only there were a battle to fight.

Washington sent Nathanael Greene south to take over command of this dire situation. Greene conducted a brilliant campaign against the British by using sneak attack tactics from the French and Indian War. Greene inflicted major damage on Cornwallis's British troops. However, the British regrouped and sent Benedict Arnold to invade Virginia.

Benedict Arnold escaped after trying to betray West Point to the British.

*Cornwallis surrendered to Washington and French commander
Rochambeau on October 17, 1781.*

First in Peace

To meet Arnold's threat and punish the traitor, Washington sent Lafayette south with a small force. Arnold retreated, leaving Lafayette to face the much larger force led by British General Cornwallis. Wisely, Lafayette skirted around the British army and avoided battle. In August, Cornwallis quartered his 7,000 troops on a peninsula at Yorktown, Virginia.

Hearing word that allied French ships were approaching Virginia, Washington combined forces with the French army, led by the Comte de Rochambeau. Together, they faked an attack on Clinton in New York. Instead, they moved south to meet the French fleet as it arrived in Virginia. Because Clinton expected the big attack to be in New York, he did not send troops to Cornwallis's aid.

The French fleet sailed to Cape Henry off Yorktown and obstructed Cornwallis's movements by sea. Washington sent Lafayette and his troops to prevent Cornwallis from moving his men off by land. Cornwallis mistakenly believed that he had been ordered to remain at Yorktown, so he made no attempt to escape the trap.

On September 15, Washington and the remainder of his forces arrived, closing the trap on Cornwallis and his men. Washington's forces laid siege to Yorktown, digging trenches, placing cannons, and tightening the noose on the British.

The Continental army's bombardment of the British forces at Yorktown began on October 9.

On October 17, Cornwallis surrendered. This victory for Washington was followed by tragedy when he learned that his stepson, Jackie, was critically ill. Washington was at his stepson's bedside when Jackie died on November 5.

In Washington's experience, the British always retaliated after defeat. Clinton was still in command of his portion of the British army in New York, and other British troops lingered in the colonies. Washington did not believe that the British had given up, so he kept his army together. However, the British had lost the will to fight. In 1783, the British signed the Treaty of Paris and recognized the independent nation of the United States of America. The Revolutionary War was over.

When the war began, Washington had not been an experienced military strategist, and he made a number of tactical errors. Yet, over the course of the eight-year struggle, he showed himself to be an inspired leader. He was levelheaded, determined in the worst of circumstances, and he learned from his mistakes. Washington never gave up. Then, his goals accomplished, Washington did what many great military leaders could not: he surrendered his power willingly for the benefit of his country.

Washington longed to go home to his estate, Mount Vernon.

Home to Mount Vernon

After so many years of war, Washington wanted nothing more than to return home to his wife and his farm. Yet, a quiet retirement was not Washington's destiny, and he had much work to do. From his experiences during the Revolutionary War, Washington knew that the country needed a stronger central government. The national government had little power and no way to pay its debts.

Some who were frustrated with the Continental Congress called for Washington to become king.

Although Washington had his own frustrations with the Continental Congress, he did not believe that the United States needed a king, nor did he want to be that monarch. He believed that total power for one person was contrary to the principles of the American Revolution.

The Electoral College

Washington was elected unanimously, with 69 votes, to be the first president of the United States. During that election, the majority of people were not allowed to vote for president. The only votes that counted were those of the electoral college. The electoral college was made up of representatives from each state.

Later, the electoral college system changed. Today, people across the country cast votes for the president. However, the people's votes are still not counted directly. Instead, each state has delegates in the electoral college. The delegates, or electors, are pledged to vote for whichever presidential candidate wins in their state. In 2008, there were a total of 538 electors in the electoral college. A candidate needed to receive 270 votes to win the presidency.

The electoral college system has caused confusion sometimes because it is possible for a candidate to win the electoral college vote but lose the popular vote. This happened most recently in 2000 when George W. Bush became president.

THE CONSTITUTIONAL CONVENTION

A convention to revise the new country's system of government was scheduled for May 1787. Many Virginians wanted Washington to lead their state's delegation to the convention. Washington refused at first, but his friends convinced him to attend.

Twelve states sent representatives to Philadelphia for the convention.

The delegates met in what is now called Independence Hall and unanimously voted for Washington to be president of the convention. After much discussion, the delegates came to recognize that they needed a new document to govern the nation. After months of meetings and debate, they accepted a draft of the Constitution of the United States. Next, the Constitution had to be ratified by at least nine states to become the law of the land. Ultimately, every state ratified the Constitution.

The Constitution called for an electoral college of representatives from each state to elect the president. The electoral college voted unanimously to elect Washington as the first president of the United States. John Adams became vice president. Excited crowds watched on April 30, 1789, as Washington placed his hand on the Bible and solemnly swore to execute the office of the president and uphold the Constitution of the United States.

PRESIDENT OF THE UNITED STATES

Washington served two successful terms as president. His leadership helped formulate the

Washington DC

Washington is the only U.S. president in history who did not reside in the White House. The White House was not yet constructed during Washington's presidency, and Washington DC was not the capital of the United States.

The first capital was in New York City. Later, the capital was housed in Philadelphia. Washington worked on the White House, the capitol building, and the new capital city. In 1800, Washington DC became the capital of the United States. The city was named after George Washington.

structure of the executive branch that exists today. He was well aware that his actions and decisions likely would have historic consequences. Washington set up a cabinet system to receive the counsel of his most trusted advisors. As he had done during the war, he surrounded himself with bright, able statesmen and delegated authority to them.

Washington helped the 13 separate states become more united as a nation. He appointed people from many different states to posts in his government, and he visited every state in his first term in office. Washington backed Congress in establishing the Bill of Rights that guaranteed the freedom of speech, freedom of religion, freedom of the press, and many other individual rights. He also helped create the nation's system of courts of law.

Despite major debate and controversy, Washington worked with Alexander Hamilton as secretary of the treasury to repay war debts and push for changes in the country's financial system. The Constitution called for Congress to establish a seat of government. After great discussion and bargaining, a location on the Potomac River was chosen. Design and construction began on the new capital city, Washington DC.

A SECOND TERM

Washington was unanimously elected to a second term as president and was sworn in on March 4, 1793. He faced many challenging issues during his second term. Disagreements rose up between members of the Federalist Party, who believed in a stronger federal government, and members of the Democratic-Republican Party, who believed in personal liberties and a weaker centralized government.

The French Revolution began in 1789 and brought France and Great Britain to war once more in 1793. Some U.S. leaders worried that the French Revolution would lead to the collapse of other governments, even that of the United States. Other leaders applauded the revolution as an expansion of people's freedom. The United States had to decide whether to support one side or another. Some

First Lady

Martha Washington fol-
lowed her husband to
various homes in the
temporary capitals of
New York City and Phila-
delphia. As wife of the
president, she entertained
all the guests formally, not
wanting European visitors
to think that Americans
were rustic. However,
those who were close to
her found her to be warm
and friendly. From her
letters, it seems that she
found her new life more
of a duty than a privi-
lege, and she was happy
to return to Mount Ver-
non. After George died in
1799, Martha burned all
their letters to each other
because she wanted them
to stay private. She died
in 1802.

Americans, including Declaration
of Independence author Thomas
Jefferson, argued for the United
States to support France and oppose
Great Britain once more. Others,
including Hamilton, believed that
the nation needed trade ties with the
British. Washington wanted to stay
out of foreign wars entirely and kept
the United States out of the conflict.
He knew that the new nation was in
no position to start another war, no
matter the principle behind it.

Other major conflicts and
crises challenged the new nation.
After eight years in the presidency,
Washington decided to retire and
drafted a farewell address. In 1796,
Washington's famous farewell address
was printed in publications across
the land. In it, Washington urged the
American people to come together as
a nation and view their differences as
a strength. He asserted:

The very idea of the power and right of the People to establish Government presupposes the duty of every Individual to obey the established government.[1]

He believed that, since the people had founded the government and participated in it, every individual had the responsibility to follow the law.

RETIREMENT

In March 1797, the reins of government were handed over to the newly elected president, John Adams, and vice president, Thomas Jefferson.

Washington and Martha returned to Mount Vernon. Washington remained busy, working on the new capital, overseeing repairs at the estate, riding out to his farms, hosting numerous visitors and dignitaries, and attending to his correspondence. Washington was called back to duty as commander in chief of the army when war with France threatened, but diplomacy settled the crisis and he did not have to serve.

Washington routinely rode around his estate. On December 12, 1799, he set forth into snowy, rainy weather. He was soaked and cold but had dinner guests waiting for him so he did not change his clothing when he got home. The next day, despite a sore throat, Washington walked around his property to mark trees he wanted cut. That night, when he had trouble breathing, doctors were summoned.

Washington suffered through the primitive medical treatments of the day, but he finally told the doctors to stop. He stated, "I die hard, but I am not afraid to go."[2] Commander to the end, Washington checked his own pulse before taking his final breaths. On December 14, 1799, at the age of 67, George Washington died. The nation mourned as many praised their former commander and president. The sentiments of Henry Lee, one of Washington's cavalry officers, are still remembered. He declared that Washington was "First in war, first in peace, and first in the hearts of his countrymen."[3]

Final Resting Place

Congress built a vault underneath the Capitol building specifically to house Washington's body. However, Washington objected to this plan. He expressly stated his wish to be buried at Mount Vernon. His wishes were honored, and the vault beneath the Capitol in Washington DC remains empty.

Washington's leadership guided the founding of the United States.

TIMELINE

1732	1743	1748
Washington is born in Westmoreland County, Virginia, on February 22.	Washington's father dies.	Washington takes his first job as a surveyor.

1759	1774	1775
Washington marries Martha Dandridge Custis on January 6.	Washington is selected as a delegate to the First Continental Congress.	Washington is appointed commander of the Continental army.

1752	1754	1754
Washington's half-brother Lawrence dies in July, and Washington takes a position in the militia.	The French and Indian War begins after Washington and Half-King attack a group of French soldiers.	Washington surrenders Fort Necessity in July.

1776	1776	1776
In March, Washington takes Dorchester Heights and drives the British out of Boston.	In the fall, Washington retreats from New York City.	On December 26, Washington defeats the Hessian force at Trenton.

TIMELINE

1777	1777	1777–1778
On January 3, Washington defeats the British at Princeton.	Washington loses battles at Brandywine on September 11 and Germantown on October 4.	Washington and his troops survive the winter at Valley Forge.

1787	1789	1793
Washington is elected president of the Constitutional Convention.	Washington is elected the first president of the United States.	Washington is reelected to a second term as president.

1778	1781	1783
In February, the French formalize an alliance with the Patriots.	British troops surrender at the Battle of Yorktown on October 17.	The American Revolution officially ends with the Treaty of Paris.

1796	1797	1799
Washington publishes his Farewell Address.	Washington retires and relinquishes power to newly elected president John Adams in March.	Washington dies on December 14 at the age of 67.

ESSENTIAL FACTS

DATE OF BIRTH

February 22, 1732

PLACE OF BIRTH

Westmoreland County, Virginia

DATE OF DEATH

December 14, 1799

PARENTS

Augustine Washington and Mary Ball Washington

EDUCATION

Tutor

MARRIAGE

Martha Dandridge Custis, January 6, 1759

CHILDREN

Stepchildren Martha (Patsy) and John (Jackie)

CAREER HIGHLIGHTS

Washington was commander in chief of the Continental army in the Revolutionary War. He contributed to the founding principles and documents of the nation and became the first president of the United States.

SOCIETAL CONTRIBUTION

Early lessons learned fighting alongside the British helped guide Washington to defeat one of the greatest military forces of the day and win the American Revolution. Leading the Continental army convinced Washington of the need for a strong central U.S. government. Washington established the principle that the military would obey the political leaders in the United States. Washington could have been king, yet he insisted on a democratic government. Washington's humility and sacrifice inspired greatness in others in serving the country.

CONFLICTS

French and Indian War, Revolutionary War

QUOTE

"First in war, first in peace, and first in the hearts of his countrymen."—*Henry Lee*

ADDITIONAL RESOURCES

SELECT BIBLIOGRAPHY

Brookhiser, Richard. *Founding Father: Rediscovering George Washington.* New York, NY: The Free Press, 1996.

Burns, James MacGregor, and Susan Dunn. *George Washington.* New York, NY: Henry Holt and Company, 2004.

Ellis, Joseph J. *His Excellency George Washington.* New York, NY: Vintage Books, 2004.

McCullough, David. *1776.* New York, NY: Simon & Schuster, 2006.

FURTHER READING

Calkhoven, Laurie. *George Washington: An American Life.* New York, NY: Sterling Publishing Company, 2006.

Freedman, Russell. *Washington at Valley Forge.* New York, NY: Holiday House, 2008.

Marrin, Albert. *George Washington and the Founding of a Nation.* New York, NY: Dutton Juvenile, 2001.

West, David, and Jackie Gaff. *George Washington: The Life of an American Patriot.* New York, NY: Rosen Publishing Group, 2005.

Web Links

To learn more about George Washington, visit ABDO Publishing Company online at **www.abdopublishing.com**. Web sites about George Washington are featured on our Book Links page. These links are routinely monitored and updated to provide the most current information available.

Places to Visit

Mount Vernon
Historic Mount Vernon
3200 Mount Vernon Memorial Highway, Mount Vernon, VA 22309
703-780-2000
www.mountvernon.org
Washington's estate is now a museum open to the public and features living history reenactments.

National Archives Experience
Constitution Ave. NW (between 7th & 9th Streets)
Washington, DC 20408
202-357-5450
www.archives.gov/nae/visit
View the U.S. Constitution, Bill of Rights, and Declaration of Independence in the Rotunda for the Charters of Freedom. The Archives also feature exhibits and guided tours.

University of Virginia
The Papers of George Washington
504 Alderman Library, Charlottesville, VA 22904
434-924-3569
gwpapers.virginia.edu
The University of Virginia houses documents, papers, and articles relating to our first president.

GLOSSARY

artillery
Large guns that are moved on wheels.

bayonet
A long blade fixed on the end of a rifle.

boycott
An effort to have no dealings with a person, an organization, a store, or a country, typically done to express disapproval or influence something to change.

constitution
A document of the basic principles and laws of a nation or state.

delegate
A representative at an assembly or convention.

fortification
Defensive walls.

Loyalist
During the American Revolution, a colonist who remained loyal to Great Britain.

militia
A group of citizens organized into an army.

musket
A heavy handheld gun carried by individual soldiers in the seventeenth and eighteenth centuries.

Patriot
>	During the American Revolution, a colonist who rebelled against Great Britain and supported American independence.

petition
>	A written request to a government or leader.

ratify
>	To make into law.

repeal
>	To take back or undo.

representation
>	Having members of a government who speak for a specific group or area.

revolution
>	The overthrow of a ruler or government by citizens.

sentries
>	Soldiers who guard a military camp.

siege
>	A type of battle in which one force is trapped in a city or within walls by another force.

strategist
>	A person who uses logic, knowledge, and experience to make a plan.

survey
>	To analyze and measure the land.

treason
>	An act of betrayal against one's country or leaders.

Source Notes

Chapter 1. "His Excellency"
1. Joseph J. Ellis. *His Excellency George Washington*. New York, NY: Random House, 2004. 136.
2. Willard Sterne Randall. *George Washington: A Life*. New York, NY: Henry Holt, 1997. 393.

Chapter 2. A Child of Virginia
1. "The Papers of George Washington Digital Edition." *University of Virginia Press*. 30 June 2009 <http://rotunda.upress.virginia.edu:8080/pgwde/dflt.xqy?mode=menu>.
2. Ibid.
3. "Text from George Washington's Journal." *Archiving Early America*. 22 August 2009 <http://www.earlyamerica.com/earlyamerica/milestones/journal/journaltext.html>.

Chapter 3. First Battles
1. Joseph J. Ellis. *His Excellency George Washington*. New York, NY: Random House, 2004. 14–15.

Chapter 4. Command
None

Chapter 5. Taxation without Representation
1. Patrick Henry. "Give Me Liberty or Give Me Death." 23 Mar. 1775. *earlyamerica.com*. 2 Jul. 2009 <http://www.earlyamerica.com/earlyamerica/bookmarks/henry/speech.htm>.
2. James MacGregor Burns and Susan Dunn. *George Washington*. New York, NY: Henry Holt, 2004. 23.
3. Ibid. 24.

Chapter 6. Commander in Chief
1. David McCullough. *1776*. New York, NY: Simon & Schuster, 2006. 95.
2. Ibid. 52.
3. Ibid. 25.
4. Ibid. 105.
5. Ibid. 135.
6. James MacGregor Burns and Susan Dunn. *George Washington*. New York, NY: Henry Holt, 2004. 26.
7. James Thomas Flexner. *George Washington in the American Revolution (1775–1873)*. Boston, MA: Little, Brown and Company, 1967, 1968. 97.

Source Notes Continued

Chapter 7. Attack on New York
1. David McCullough. *1776.* New York, NY: Simon & Schuster, 2006. 193.
2. Ibid. 145–146.
3. Ibid. 177.

Chapter 8. A Defensive War
1. David McCullough. *1776.* New York, NY: Simon & Schuster, 2006. 224.

Chapter 9. The Army Survives
1. Joseph J. Ellis. *His Excellency George Washington.* New York, NY: Random House, 2004. 117.
2. Ibid. 112.
3. Ibid. 123.
4. Ibid. 111.

Chapter 10. First in Peace
1. Joseph J. Ellis. *His Excellency George Washington.* New York, NY: Random House, 2004. 236.
2. John E. Ferling. *The First of Men, A Life of George Washington.* Knoxville, TN: The University of Tennessee Press, 1988. 506.
3. Joseph J. Ellis. *His Excellency George Washington.* New York, NY: Random House, 2004. 270.

INDEX

INDEX CONTINUED

ABOUT THE AUTHOR

Sari Earl is an attorney. After winning first place in a writing competition, she began a full-time writing career. In addition to published novels of adult-level fiction, she's written articles and young adult books. She writes fiction and nonfiction and enjoys the challenge of both. Her books have been published in countries around the world. She lives with her family in Atlanta, Georgia.

PHOTO CREDITS